THE GHOSTLY TALES OF FLORIDA'S HAUNTED LIGHTHOUSES

Published by Arcadia Children's Books
A Division of Arcadia Publishing, Inc.
Charleston, SC
www.arcadiapublishing.com

Copyright © 2025 by Arcadia Children's Books
All rights reserved

Spooky America is a trademark of Arcadia Publishing, Inc.

First published 2025
Manufactured in the United States

Designed by Jessica Nevins
Images used courtesy of Shutterstock.com.

ISBN: 9781467197731
Library of Congress Control Number: 2024939047

Notice: The information in this book is true and complete to the best of our knowledge. It is offered without guarantee on the part of the author or Arcadia Publishing. The author and Arcadia Publishing disclaim all liability in connection with the use of this book.

All rights reserved. No part of this book may be reproduced or transmitted in any form whatsoever without prior written permission from the publisher except in the case of brief quotations embodied in critical articles and reviews.

Spooky America

THE GHOSTLY TALES OF FLORIDA'S HAUNTED LIGHTHOUSES

DAN ALLEVA

Adapted from *Haunted Florida Lighthouses* by Heather Leigh, PhD

arcadia
CHILDREN'S BOOKS

Table of Contents & Map Key

Welcome to Florida's Spooky Lighthouses!. 3

Chapter 1. Why are Florida's Lighthouses So Spooky?. 7

1 Chapter 2. St. Augustine Lighthouse 13

2 Chapter 3. St. Johns River Light 21

3 Chapter 4. Port Boca Grande Lighthouse. 29

Chapter 5. Cape Florida Lighthouse. 37

4 Chapter 6. Jupiter Inlet Lighthouse 45

5 Chapter 7. Key West Lighthouse 51

6 Chapter 8. Sanibel Island Lighthouse. 59

7 Chapter 9. Cedar Key (Seahorse Key) Lighthouse 65

Chapter 10. Mount Dora Lighthouse 75

8 Chapter 11. Egmont Key Lighthouse 81

9 Chapter 12. Garden Key Light 87

10 Chapter 13. Ponce de Leon Inlet Light 95

11 Chapter 14. Carysfort Reef Light. 101

A Ghostly Goodbye 107

Welcome to Florida's Spooky Lighthouses!

Want to know a secret about Florida that most tourists miss? Sure, millions of people come to splash in the waves and build sandcastles on the powder-white sand. But the REAL Florida adventures aren't happening on those crowded shores—they're towering above them! From the historic streets of St. Augustine to the windswept Keys, Florida's coastline is dotted with incredible lighthouses. These enormous towers have stood guard over the Gulf of Mexico to the west and the mighty Atlantic Ocean to the east for hundreds of years. And trust me, they've seen things that would make your jaw drop. These aren't just tall, pretty buildings—they're time machines filled with epic stories just waiting to be discovered!

The famous English author Virginia Woolf praised lighthouses for what she believed was their similarities with human beings. She saw them as lonely figures, much like the keepers who operated them, providing guidance to ships along the ocean. Keepers lived in or close to the light towers, often with their families. Long before tourists rushed to Florida to have fun in the sun, these essential watchers of the seas kept guard over Florida's waters. Often, lighthouse keepers and their families would spend weeks, if not months, in these towers of isolation. This was especially true during the American Civil War, when their strategic positions put Florida's lighthouses in the path of conflict.

Florida lighthouses and their keepers

were disconnected from the mainland. This meant the keepers didn't always receive key information needed to stay safe. They were often in harm's way. Given this dramatic history, it's no surprise that Florida lighthouses harbor many mysteries ... and maybe even ghosts!

Yep, you heard that right: the more you learn about them, the more you'll discover that there are *many* reports of supernatural activity in and around these haunting—and maybe even haunted—landmarks. So grab your detective hat and flashlight, because we're about to uncover some seriously spooky stuff. This book is *packed* with spine-tingling tales of things that go bump in the night (and sometimes broad daylight) around these beacons by the sea. Of course, these tales of shadows and specters are not meant to make you believe in the paranormal— that is up to you to decide. Are you brave enough to keep reading? Let's dive in and find out!

Why are Florida's Lighthouses So Spooky?

Today, thirty working lighthouses sit along the 1,800 miles of Florida's coastline. Many other lighthouses, no longer in operation, still stand as historical landmarks on the state's shores. In fact, Florida has named more lighthouses as historical landmarks than any other state in America. It's hard to say with certainty that every lighthouse in Florida is haunted, but it also can't be ruled out. However, this much is true: authorities have received reports of the paranormal at nearly *every* lighthouse in Florida.

Perhaps it's not surprising that ghosts are said to lurk in or near lighthouses. In a way, lighthouses are like superheroes of the sea. Their job? To keep ships safe from jagged rocks, dangerous storms, and even vicious pirates (shiver me timbers!). With all that action and danger, it's no wonder some spooky roommates might've decided to stick

around. Many visitors report strange creaks and groans, as if the lighthouse is trying to tell them a secret. Others swear they've seen strange shadows, glowing orbs, and even ghostly figures wandering in and around these mysterious seaside landmarks.

But what *is* it about lighthouses that makes them such spirit magnets? Why do ghost hunters and paranormal experts pick up so many spooky signals and supernatural activity in these towers by the sea? Some people believe that spirits often return to the place they once called home. (With those stunning ocean views from dusk until dawn, can you really blame them?) Others say that renovations to a historic structure like a lighthouse can "awaken" the spirits of the people who once lived there—all that drilling and construction causing a bit of a spooky shake up!

But not everyone agrees that lighthouses are as haunted as they seem. Some people believe that those who have had "eerie experiences" are either making them up or imagining they are seeing something that's not really there. In the old days, lighthouses were lit with gas lamps. Burning these lamps created carbon monoxide, an odorless, colorless gas that can cause illness or even death if inhaled, but can *also* make people hallucinate, or see things that aren't really there. Is it possible that the keepers who reported ghostly apparitions were just hallucinating? Or, did they truly have a brush with the paranormal?

We may never know the real reason that Florida's lighthouses are so spooky. But what we *do* know is that you are sure to find the stories about them facinating. Whether you believe in ghosts or not, the lighthouse legends in this book are guaranteed to give you goosebumps. From Florida's serene Gulf Coast shores to the wild waves of its Atlantic seaboard, you may never look at the Sunshine State the same way again!

St. Augustine Lighthouse

St. Augustine Lighthouse

The St. Augustine Lighthouse is not just the oldest lighthouse in Florida—it's the oldest lighthouse in the United States! Built between 1871 and 1874, it sits on Anastasia Island, just north of St. Augustine Beach, where the Matanzas and Tolomato Rivers empty into the Atlantic Ocean. At 164 feet tall (about half the height of the Statue of Liberty), the

St. Augustine Lighthouse is listed on the National Register of Historic Places and home to a naval museum. But visitors beware: the chances of running into a ghost here are extremely high! In fact, so many ghosts inside the St. Augustine Lighthouse, no one really knows how many there are. No *wonder* locals say it's the most haunted lighthouse in all of Florida!

Originally built by the Spanish army as a lookout tower to detect pirates (shiver me timbers!), it became a lighthouse after many decades. In the beginning, the lighthouse operated using a series of lamps and reflective mirrors to cast light out into the evening sky. However, this method wasn't successful, and ships still had difficulty navigating the dark waters of the Atlantic Ocean.

Powerful lenses that projected strong light

became available in the nineteenth century, but they were very expensive. The tower was raised ten feet so its light could be seen farther out at sea, but the extension didn't help much. Finally, in 1874, the lighthouse was fitted with more proper equipment: a Fresnel lens. Invented by French engineer, Augustin Jean Fresnel, this lens advanced the capability of lighthouses forever, including the St. Augustine Lighthouse, and is known as the invention that saved a million ships. The lens is still in place today.

The first reported haunting here happened in 1876. That year, the lighthouse keeper's quarters burned in a mysterious fire. Thankfully, the quarters were not in use at the time and no one was injured. The remains of the house lay untouched until this part of St. Augustine became a National Historic

Landmark District. A renovation project started, intended to restore the St. Augustine Lighthouse to its original beauty.

But there was one small problem: as the hammers, saws, and plows began to chip away at the remains, they unleashed tons of sleepy specters!

You see—as any paranormal expert will tell you—even the simplest of renovations can awaken spirits from their slumber inside gravel and stone. Ghosts are a bit like humans. Mostly, they want to spend their days in the afterlife in peace—not with a wrecking ball smashing through the walls! Given all the hauntings reported here over the years, it seems the ghosts at the St. Augustine Lighthouse are intent on *never* letting the living forget the mistake they made in restoring the quarters, no matter how good the intentions were!

From the beginning, the restoration project seemed to be cursed. Reports began to surface of a "demon" determined to scare workers from their posts. In fact, this so-called demon succeeded in frightening away many workers, while others simply ignored the paranormal activity that seemed to plague the workplace. One man—Hezekiah T. Pittee—carried on with his business at St. Augustine Lighthouse, only to pay the ultimate price.

Pittee was the project leader at the lighthouse, which meant he was in charge of nearly every aspect of the building. The two eldest of his three daughters, Eliza and Mary, came to work with their father at the St. Augustine Lighthouse quite often. But one day, tragedy struck: while riding around the grounds in a work vehicle, the girls lost control and toppled into the water, where they drowned. They were just thirteen and fifteen at the time.

But it would appear the Pittees haven't moved far from the St. Augustine Lighthouse, even in the afterlife. Today, staff and visitors speak of "playful spirits" that inhabit the lighthouse. Many believe these are the ghosts of the departed Pittee girls. Bizarre occurrences happen here, like the sound of children laughing, even when none can be seen. There's even a musical box that pops open and turns on by itself!

That's not all—some visitors to the lighthouse believe they have seen ghosts of little girls, their small faces peeking through the windows when the lighthouse is supposed to be empty. There are reports of ghostly laughter at a nearby swing set on the grounds.

One visitor even claimed to see the apparition of a small girl playing on the swing.

However, if the Pittee sisters have returned to the St. Augustine Lighthouse, they are not alone. Activity tends to pick up when tours are happening at the lighthouse. Many visitors have reported the feeling of being touched by unseen hands. An employee once described having locked the door to the lighthouse tower the night before, only to find it sitting wide open in the morning!

Should you ever visit the St. Augustine Lighthouse, expect the unexpected. If you happen to encounter a ghost, just do what the staff at the lighthouse do and play it cool. While they're far from shy, the ghosts here seem friendly.

That's not the case at every lighthouse!

St. Johns River Light

The magnitude of the St. Johns River is most impressive. For more than three hundred miles, it runs through alligator-infested swamps, stunning cypress tree forests, crystal-clear springs, and vast wetlands as far as the eye can see. Its gentle northward flow makes it unique: most rivers flow southward. Outdoor enthusiasts and water sport lovers get their thrills on the extending waterways of the St. Johns River, which is also the largest, widest, and laziest river in all Florida.

But beyond the gators, manatees, and even sharks that call the St. Johns River home, it may *also* be home to a deadly deep-sea, prehistoric monster! No, your eyes did not deceive you. This is the story of the St. Johns Monster, a deadly sea demon with the build of a dinosaur that rises up from the muddy depths with a hunger for the greatest prey of all: *US!*

Though proof of the St. Johns Monster's existence is murky, at best (no pun intended), the legend of the beast is well known in this part of Florida. The earliest sightings date back to 1953, when *The Orlando Sentinel* ran a story

about a monster reported to lurk in the St. Johns River system, from Lake Monroe all the way up to Lake George. Those who claimed to have seen the beast described it as gray in color with a horn on its head, and close to thirty-five feet long!

One river guide described the monster's head popping up out of the water near his boat during a fishing trip. "He looked at us for about a minute," the man said, "then went under the water and swam away from us. We waited about two hours in that same spot to see if he would come up again, but he didn't."

From there, rumors of the beast only grew. Some people said they'd seen a terrifying reptilian creature while swimming, fishing, or boating. Others talked about its "monstrous" appetite for water hyacinth, a floating plant with blue and purple flowers found in nearly all Florida's lakes and rivers.

At one point, a group of daring locals even planned a monster hunt, hoping to catch the creature and prove it wasn't just a tall tale.

Still, not everyone believed the rumors. In fact, local scientists had a much simpler explanation: They said people had probably mistaken dolphins and manatees for the monster, and then exaggerated the details about what they'd seen to make their stories more exciting. (Or maybe they'd made the stories up altogether!)

In a way, this tale is not new. Perhaps you have heard of the most famous sea creature of all, the Loch Ness Monster of Scotland (or Nessie, for short). Its existence has also been debated for decades. Some people claim they've seen the monster with their very own eyes, while others insist the story is made up.

What do *you* think?

Like the fabled Nessie, could there REALLY

be a prehistoric beast stalking the St. Johns River and its adjoining lakes? Or . . . could that strange and terrifying shadow in the water just be a fish or friendly manatee?

We may never know for sure.

What we *do* know is that some people say they've seen the St. Johns Monster not far from the St. Johns River Light. Which only makes visiting this historic spot even creepier!

The lighthouse itself was initially built in 1830, but as you now know, storm surges can be cruel to these magnificent structures. Five years after it was completed, that first lighthouse was torn down and another was rebuilt. This time, the structure was set a few miles up the shoreline to protect the lighthouse in its battle against the elements. But that proved ineffective.

By 1850, the second St. Johns River Light had become so badly battered that it was deemed unusable. A sand dune that had formed around the tower was so tall that it blocked the lighthouse for view of ships on the horizon. Once again, the St. Johns River Light was torn down and rebuilt.

This time the lighthouse was built higher and even farther inland to help protect it from rough seas and storms. Though it was decommissioned in 1929, the remains of the third and final lighthouse still stand today, located on the grounds of a naval base. But some believe there's even more to this historic landmark than meets the eye. Something... *supernatural.*

Imagine climbing the cramped, twisty staircase up to the old balcony and suddenly hearing mysterious footsteps when nobody else is there. Or feeling like someone's eyes are on you, watching from the eerie shadows, with every step you take. Pretty creepy, right?

But that's not all. Some locals and visitors swear they've even spotted ghostly figures and spectral forms wandering the nearby beaches or lurking around the lighthouse grounds.

Mighty spooky, indeed.

From lighthouse ghosts to menacing monsters splashing in the waves, you never know what you might run into when exploring this part of Florida. So keep your eyes peeled. Because whether you're climbing creaky lighthouse stairs or dipping your toes into the St. Johns, you might just find something otherworldly. That is…unless it finds you first!

Port Boca Grande Lighthouse

When you picture a lighthouse, what comes to mind? Probably *not* the Port Boca Grande Lighthouse, which looks more like a quaint and cozy beach cottage than a typical lighthouse standing tall against the sea. But looks, of course, can be deceiving, and the Port Boca Grande is no exception! Sitting at the southern tip of Gasparilla Island (just north of the Gulf Coast cities of Fort Meyers and Naples), this little lighthouse has played a big role in Florida's rich maritime history. Not to mention—Florida's *haunted* history!

Built in 1890 and one of only six Florida lighthouses that remain open to the public, the Port Boca Grande initially served to guide ships safely into and out of the Charlotte Harbor. Visitors can enter the lighthouse museum and learn about its and Gasparilla Island's interesting history. At times, it seems, things got a little *carried* away at the Port Boca Grande Lighthouse.

Gasparilla Island was once the home of the Calusa, a powerful Indigenous people who lived along the shores of Florida's southwest coast and used shells to make jewelry, tools, and other utensils. Later, Gasparilla Island became a major supplier of phosphorus—a chemical element found in rocks and on the ocean floor. It could be used to make everything from baking soda to fireworks. The island also hosted many famous and important people through the years. It was once a retreat for the rich and famous of the early twentieth century. William Lester, the lighthouse keeper from 1894 to 1923, reportedly invited millionaires like John Jacob Astor and John D. Rockefeller to stay on Gasparilla Island, likely with more luxury accommodations than one can imagine!

But William Lester invited many local guests to stay, too. With so many people passing through the area, it's no surprise that many spirits call the island and the Port Boca Grande Lighthouse home. Visitors have reported hearing some pretty odd things, such as ghostly voices, eerie laughter, and even phantom music—each phenomenon without a single reasonable explanation. Could they be the spirits of long ago simply remembering all the happy times? Perhaps they enjoyed the lighthouse keeper's parties so much, they decided to stick around... *forever?*

It seems one former resident of Gasparilla Island might have taken ghostly mischief to a whole new level. He's certainly let ghoulish mayhem go to his... head, some might say. The pirate José Gaspar is believed to be the man Gasparilla Island is named after. Many experts claim Gaspar buried his treasure and riches on the island before the lighthouse was built.

As the story goes, Jose was madly in love with Josefa, a Spanish princess. But unfortunately, the feeling was *not* mutual. In fact, Josefa made it clear numerous times that she could never love a ruthless pirate such as José. This infuriated José! He decided that if he could not win Josefa's love, he would *steal* it by kidnapping the princess. And yet, Josefa still denied José her love.

Well, that was one rejection too many for the evil pirate. In one quick instant, he drew his sword from his side and cut off Josefa's head! He then took her body and buried it on Gasparilla Island. But because his love for Josefa was so strong, he could not part with her head, and walked around with it for the rest of his days.

One word: GROSS!

Fortunately, the Port Boca Grande Lighthouse has enjoyed a solid and sturdy presence on Gasparilla Island since the dark days of decapitations. In 1972, management of the lighthouse was transferred to the county. In 1980, after years of beach erosion and neglect, the lighthouse finally got a touch up and was added to the National Register of Historic Places. In 1988, after more than twenty years, the lighthouse was relit to serve as a Coast Guard post.

But the tragedy of Princess Josefa and the ruthless pirate José has not been forgotten, and it's possible Josefa herself is still making sure of that from the afterlife. Some island locals say a headless woman roams the property, searching for ... you guessed it ... her head. Is it Josefa? No one can be sure. (Though it would certainly be ironic to have a *different* ghost missing a head roaming around the same lighthouse, wouldn't you think?)

So, should you come across the headless body of Josefa—and you're not totally petrified by her presence—maybe offer to help her search. After all, one head is better than... *none*?

Cape Florida Lighthouse

All lighthouses have a story to tell. Though, if lighthouses really could talk, the Cape Florida Lighthouse in Key Biscayne might have the most tales to tell out of *all* Florida's lighthouses.

Originally built in 1825 to help guide sailors safely around the Florida reef, it's no small wonder that the Cape Florida Lighthouse remains standing today. For 200 years, the lighthouse has sustained a lot of wear and tear thanks to erosion, hurricanes, physical attack, and even an explosion. It has been restored and rebuilt multiple times. Listed on the National Register of Historic Places, it stands ninety-five feet high and is fitted with a 109-step wooden spiral staircase that leads to a wrap-around balcony. For most Floridians, it is hard to imagine the Key Biscayne shoreline without the breathtaking Cape Florida Lighthouse. It is the oldest building in Miami-Dade County

and the most recognizable landmark in Cape Florida State Park.

The lighthouse and surrounding lands were the scene of frequent clashes in the late 1700s and early 1800s, typically between settlers and the local indigenous peoples. Key points in the American Civil War also took place here. Battles between warring parties were frequent, so the Cape Florida Lighthouse not only served as guardian of the coastline, but as a haven of safety—especially for the lighthouse keeper

and his family. According to historians, the first keeper of the Cape Florida Lighthouse, John Dubose, and his family, were also the very first citizens of Key Biscayne.

In 1836, war between the Seminole and the European-American settlers in Florida had reached a fever pitch. News of a massacre in New River (the area now known as Ft. Lauderdale) was beginning to spread among settlers. Many residents on the mainland of the Miami River crossed over the Biscayne Bay to the lighthouse, hoping it would offer better protection. While it was far from a fortress, fortifications were made to the lighthouse with the hope of keeping residents safe.

In July of 1836, Dubose and his family went to visit relatives in Key West. Save for a few members of the staff, the Cape Florida Lighthouse was unprotected. Perhaps sensing an opportunity, Seminole warriors attacked the lighthouse. The wooden structure was set on fire and the family cottage destroyed. Left in ruins, the Cape Florida Lighthouse remained abandoned for a decade. The constant threat of attack made repairing and operating the lighthouse nearly impossible.

It wasn't until 1846 that a new project got underway to rebuild the Cape Florida Lighthouse. The contractor in charge used brick and other materials remaining from the previous lighthouse. This made it cheaper to rebuild, but it also may have provoked paranormal activity. Some believe it may have even cursed the area forever.

During the 1860s, America fell into the Civil War. Tempers boiled over in the state of Florida. Like many Southern states, Florida had seceded (or withdrawn) from the Union in 1861, but that did not stop people who supported the Confederacy from damaging the lighthouse in acts of terror. After twenty-five years of war—not to mention countless tropical storms that had slowly eroded the exterior—the future of the Cape Florida Lighthouse remained in doubt for nearly a century.

As part of Miami's One Hundred Year celebration in 1996, the lighthouse was restored and reopened to the public. Visitors today can see the keeper's cottage, replicated to demonstrate how the Dubose family and other keepers lived over the course of time. In a way, with all of its antiques and artifacts of the era, entering the cottage feels like stepping back in time. But it seems something else from the past may have stuck around, too. Many say the cottage—as well as the existing environment—is charged with psychic energy.

Maybe even . . . a *ghostly* energy.

Both staff and visitors to the lighthouse have reported seeing shadowy figures and hearing strange sounds, especially while inside the new keeper's quarters. Could the artifacts and the land's complex history be the cause for these unexplained disturbances? It's hard to point to a more convincing reason.

To this day, Cape Florida Lighthouse remains an enigma among Florida's grandest beacons. What do you think? Are you brave enough for a visit?

Jupiter Inlet Lighthouse

About ninety miles to the north of the Cape Florida Lighthouse, you'll find the Jupiter Inlet Lighthouse. It's the most popular attraction in Jupiter, and it has seen its fair share of ghostly activity. Many believe the lighthouse was built on top of a burial ground belonging to the Indigenous peoples of the land. But is this only rumor? That depends on what you believe.

Here's what we know: the lighthouse was built in 1860 on a sand dune that had been used by many Indigenous tribes through time. The tower is 105 feet tall and 145 feet above sea level. Today, it is an impressive sight whether seen from air, land, or sea. It's worth a climb to the top of the tower to see the beautiful view of Jupiter Inlet.

But the area has a troubled history, which experts say might be the root of the paranormal activity at the lighthouse. Some

visitors have reported the spine-tingling sensation of an invisible hand touching their shoulders. They've heard strange noises and felt a sudden *chilling* drop in temperature. And while most people enjoy a trip to the gift shop, employees and visitors here have noted a gloom that hangs in the room, leaving them with an unspeakable feeling of sadness.

On one occasion, a visitor had a face-to-face encounter with a spirit at the top of the lighthouse stairs. A tall figure appeared

instantly. It had dark eye sockets and an enormous mouth! The apparition appeared to be floating, with a lower "body" described only as a blurry white mass.

The gruesome spirit then allegedly reached out a bony hand, and the visitor fainted. She had no recollection of how much time had passed between her encounter with the ghost and when she awoke.

Ghost historians believe this apparition could be the ghost of lighthouse keeper Joseph Willis, who is buried beside the keeper's quarters. His grave is next to that of his wife Katherine, and their children, who sadly died at birth. Today, not much is known about the Willis family, nor the tragedy that befell them. However, some locals believe their spirits might be responsible for the appearance in the lighthouse staircase and other eerie occurrences, including footsteps in empty passageways and strange voices in the area around the lighthouse.

Is there a more logical explanation for the bizarre happenings at Jupiter Inlet Lighthouse? Perhaps. But if it's not Joseph Willis and his family, then who—*or what*—could be responsible? As with all things supernatural, we may never know the answer.

Key West Lighthouse

The Key West Lighthouse and Museum receives thousands of visitors every year. People arrive hoping to catch a glimpse of the sunset or admire the beauty of the Gulf of Mexico. Yes, even if it means sight-seeing with a supernatural specter!

The lighthouse brings together two very powerful forces: the paranormal and nature. While some Floridians have had encounters with ghosts, almost every person living in the state has experienced the threat of hurricanes. These large, powerful storms regularly cause damage in Florida and can even be deadly. One such hurricane—the Havana Hurricane of 1846—was so treacherous that one witness described the aftermath as nothing short of "grotesque." During the Category 5-strength storm (the most dangerous rating for a hurricane), the Key West Lighthouse endured such deadly peril that many locals believe ghosts and spirits still roam nearby to this very day.

At the time of the Havana Hurricane, the population in Key West was about 1,500 people. Sadly, at least sixty people in Key West lost their lives in the storm. Reportedly, only eight buildings remained standing in the keys after the hurricane ended. But the storm's powerful winds and merciless tides had brought about something even more unnerving. Once the hurricane passed, all that was left of the nearby Whitehead Point Cemetery was a soggy and sandy open grave. As a result—in addition to the bodies of those killed in the storm—coffins and corpses from the cemetery *also* rose with the waters and were spread across nearly every inch of Key West.

Talk about gruesome.

To this day, many experts believe this to be the reason the Key West Lighthouse and the Keeper's Quarters Museum are so haunted. Given all the death and trauma the Havana Hurricane caused, it's no wonder this area is charged with paranormal energy, even all these years later. One spirit, in particular, seems

caught up in the deadly events of that terrible day.

Barbara Mabrity was an unlikely lighthouse keeper. She inherited the job from her late husband, who died from yellow fever soon after taking the position. After her husband's death, Barbara was determined to prove that she was every bit able to carry out this important duty. But when the Havana Hurricane arrived in full force, it proved to be too much for the fearless keeper and her six children.

As the storm came onto land, Barbara, her family, and a few other Key West residents fled to the lighthouse tower to seek shelter and safety. The winds were merciless, and the rain dropped down in buckets, pummeling the lighthouse exterior. Soon, the tower began to crumble. Then, the unthinkable happened: the lighthouse collapsed, and the deadly seas washed away all that remained of it forever.

Tragically, Barbara was only able to save one child in the catastrophe. She remained the keeper of these grounds and the newly constructed lighthouse for almost forty years. Toward the end of her time as the lighthouse keeper, the American Civil War was raging across the land. Though Barbara had managed to carry on after the devastating loss of her children, the pressures of war eventually became too much to bear. In 1864, at the age of eighty-two, she decided to retire. Despite her grief, she had served the Key West Lighthouse well.

Three years after her retirement, Barbara died. But some say she's still at the lighthouse today. One visitor said she felt the presence of a peculiar entity as she made her way up to the lighthouse tower. As she looked over her shoulder and down the eighty-eight steps she had just climbed, there was no one to be found. Then, as she entered the lantern room, she felt an eerie chill—odd considering it was eighty-five degrees that day!

As the woman headed back down the steps, she suddenly felt an unseen presence hug her from behind. She did not feel scared, though. Instead, it seemed that whoever (or whatever) had hugged her wasn't trying to frighten her. The woman said it actually felt like she was being *comforted* by the presence.

Other lighthouse visitors have shared similar stories. They often experience cold breezes that come from nowhere, or the feeling of having their hair touched. Some guests even claim to have *seen* the ghost of Barbara Mabrity in the stairway of the lighthouse. She is typically spotted making her way up to the top of the tower before fading away.

According to paranormal experts, Barbara's ghost may be a residual haunting—a moment in time playing over and over. As she paces through the Key West Lighthouse, she might be reliving her final days or searching endlessly for her missing children, perhaps not even realizing she has passed on. So if you happen to meet Barbara's spirt during your visit, remember: she's not there to frighten anyone. She's simply a mother whose dedication to her children—and to the lighthouse she looked after—lives on even after death.

Sanibel Island Lighthouse

On the Gulf Coast of Florida, just south of Fort Meyers, there is a thin island shaped like a crescent. Nicknamed the seashell capital of the world, Sanibel Island attracts thousands of tourists every year. But visitors to this special place might discover more than colorful seashells... they may even meet some ghosts!

One of the first lighthouses on Florida's gulf coast north of Key West, Sanibel Island

Lighthouse took some time to be built. In 1833, a small group of European settlers explored the possibility of building a lighthouse on the island. They organized a petition (a formal request signed by members of the public and submitted to the government) to request a lighthouse for the safety of passing ships, but it was rejected. Soon after, the settlers abandoned the island.

In the two decades that followed, the landscape of the United States changed rapidly. In 1862, the U.S. Congress passed a bill called the Homestead Act that allowed people to apply

to purchase government land, often called "homesteads." As a result, Sanibel Island again found itself populated with new residents. Twice more, residents petitioned to build a lighthouse, but neither attempt succeeded. In 1883, there was finally a breakthrough. The U.S. Congress approved funding to build the Sanibel Island Lighthouse. Construction began swiftly in February the following year. On August 20, 1884, the lighthouse was lit for the very first time by its first keeper, Dudley Richards. The Sanibel Island shoreline was illuminated like never before.

As the years passed, many valiant keepers would serve the lighthouse. But little by little, rumors of hauntings began to swirl. Could it be because of the frightening story associated with one-time assistant lighthouse keeper Richard T. Barry? Sadly, a man named Jesse W. Lee murdered Barry on June 26, 1919. According to the story, Barry may have insulted Lee's wife, giving Lee motive to commit the crime. Lee never denied killing Barry, only claiming that it was in self-defense. Lee was ultimately acquitted, or freed, for the charge of murder. But some say a strange presence lingers in the lighthouse, even today. Could Barry's restless spirit feel there has been no justice for his murder?

Though no one has ever officially claimed to have seen a ghost in or around the lighthouse, paranormal researchers believe that something other-worldly is happening here. For years, locals have shared stories of shadow figures, strange lights glowing from the lighthouse, eerie voices, and irregular cold spots throughout the island.

What do you think? Are you brave enough to visit the Sanibel Island Lighthouse? Could *you* be the first person to reconnect with the spirit of Richard T. Barry? It's entirely possible you might not witness anything out of the ordinary. Then again, you never know what you could discover should you find yourself on Sanibel Island at night, or what could find *you*. That eerie glow in the lighthouse window? Well, it could just be the moon. Or maybe, just maybe... it's lighthouse keeper Richard T. Barry, signaling to you from beyond the grave.

Cedar Key Lighthouse

Cedar Key (Seahorse Key) Lighthouse

Some people say that when you visit Cedar Key, it's like stepping back in time. Located sixty miles southwest of Gainesville, the small cluster of islands that make up this magical place sits three miles out into the Gulf of Mexico and is known for its incredible seafood, fishing, birdwatching, and National Wildlife Refuge. Sadly, parts of Cedar Key were destroyed in 2024 due to Hurricane Helene and other storms, and the community faces a long road of rebuilding. But the people of Cedar Key have always been resilient and strong—and the spirits said to reside here are no different!

Long before cars and iPhones existed, Indigenous peoples called these islands home. They fished in rich waters and gathered oysters and clams, and some of their shell mounds can still be seen today. In the 1800s, Cedar Key became a busy port town. Huge steamboats would chug in and out of the harbor, carrying people and goods. The town was even connected to the East Coast by Florida's first cross-state railroad in 1861.

During the Second Seminole War, from 1835 to 1842, the Navy used this area as a hospital, as well as a camp for prisoners. Important moments in the American Civil War also played out on these shores. In 1862, as intense battles between the Union and Confederate armies raged, much-needed supplies arrived by sea route. Often, lighthouses provided guidance to ships at night, when they were likely to slip in unseen.

This is true of Seahorse Key, a small island just south of the Cedar Keys channel. Seahorse Key was a cargo stop for the Union Army along the route between Key West and Saint Marks after the Union gained control of the area from the Confederates. After the war, the village of Cedar Key became known for its abundance of cedar trees (that's how Cedar Key got its name). Ships carried the wood to factories, where it was turned into pencils and other items.

The Cedar Key Lighthouse (also called Seahorse Key Lighthouse) was first lit on August 1, 1854, by keeper William Wilson. Like the St. Augustine Lighthouse, the Cedar Key Lighthouse was powered by a Fresnel lens, which made it possible for the lighthouse to be seen from farther away. Today, Seahorse Key is only accessible by boat and is part of the Cedar Keys National Wildlife Refuge. Nearly 250 bird species, including white ibis, egrets, herons, and pelicans call Seahorse Key their home. But... they're not the only ones here!

Standing at the top of Seahorse Key today are three graves belonging to former members of the U.S Navy: Ordinary Seamen Patrick Doran from Bushwick, New York; Ordinary Seaman Ephraim Hearn, from Norfolk, Virginia, and Landsman William M. Robinson from Philadelphia, Pennsylvania. These men never expected not to return home to their families. Though, as fate would have it, they all died at sea. As was customary at the time, the men were buried near where they perished. Their graves still peer out into the waters off Seahorse Key. If stories are to be believed, their spirits have never left the island and are responsible for strange happenings.

Perhaps the most famous ghost on Seahorse Key is that of a headless pirate who legend says rides a palomino horse at night. This gruesome sight is believed to be the spirit of Pierre LeBlanc, a follower of the ruthless pirate Jean Lafitte, a merciless thief and all-around bad guy.

As the story goes, long ago, Lafitte left LeBlanc on Seahorse Key with a palomino and supplies and put LeBlanc in charge of guarding the buried treasure the men had just hidden on the island. It's more than likely that Lafitte and LeBlanc both presumed that LeBlanc was the only one on the island at the time. However, they were wrong. *Dead* wrong—as LeBlanc would soon learn.

One day, LeBlanc came across a stranger. Surprised to find he wasn't alone, LeBlanc took up conversation with this curious vagabond. That was his first mistake, but it was his second mistake that cost LeBlanc his life. Later in the evening, LeBlanc began to drink and eventually became very loose-lipped. Astoundingly, he revealed the location of the treasure to his new "friend." This was all the stranger needed. That evening, the stranger stole all of Jean Lafitte's treasure. When LeBlanc awoke to find what had happened, he attacked the stranger. But the battle was not even close. With a swish of his sword, the mysterious islander removed LeBlanc's head with precision. (A gruesome end for LeBlanc, 'tis true, but Jean Lafitte would likely have done the same thing when he learned LaBlanc had lost his treasure!)

Along with a headless pirate, Seahorse Key is also said to be home to a ghost dog and the spirit of its owner, Annie Simpson. Some claim to have seen glowing ghostly visions in the woods near the island's famed Shell Mound Trail, part of the Lower Suwannee Wildlife Refuge—the same place where Annie and her dog are believed to have lost their lives. Centuries ago, this area of swampland and woods was known as a favorite treasure-hiding spot for pirates (yes, just like Jean

Lafitte and his headless associate, LeBlanc). As the story goes, young Annie Simpson and her wolfhound often roamed these woods, picking berries and wildflowers despite warnings of pirates afoot. Until one day, when the pair vanished, never to be seen again.

Some believe Annie and her dog stumbled across something in the woods they shouldn't have—like pirates burying their treasure—and paid a dear price, indeed. Over the years, explorers have discovered mysterious artifacts on the island: scattered caches of old coins dating back centuries and, most eerily, the intact skeleton of a very large dog. But because Annie's body was never found, her true fate remains a mystery. Some say this is why her restless spirit still roams these woods, waiting for someone to find her and finally bring her peace.

From headless pirates to glowing visions to ghost dogs, the gruesome events of the past seem to have left their mark on Seahorse Key. Perhaps that's why paranormal experts say this lonely island, full of so many restless spirits, may not be so lonely after all ...

Mount Dora Lighthouse

You have read about the lighthouses that line the east and west coasts of Florida. But would you be surprised to find there is a lighthouse in Florida that does not call either of these two coastlines home? If your answer is yes, you may never have heard of Mount Dora Lighthouse, located in the center of the state along the shores of Lake Dora in Mount Dora, Florida.

Mount Dora is a charming town known for its historic buildings, antique shops, beautiful canopy oak trees, and small-town southern charm. Nicknamed "Festival City," Mount Dora hosts more than thirty festivals a year, including the Mount Dora Arts Festival, the Antique and Classic Boat Festival, the Steampunk Industrial Show, and Georgefest, the longest running festival in Florida celebrating the birthday of George Washington. Lake Dora is also a popular tourist destination. Visitors waterski, wakeboard, and soak up the sun along the waterways and shore where the small but mighty Mount Dora Lighthouse can be found.

Standing at only thirty-five feet tall, the red-and-white striped Mount Dora Lighthouse is the only inland freshwater lighthouse in the entire state of Florida. It may not tower over its town like lighthouses found along coastal waters, but this charming little lighthouse has played an important role for Central Florida's series of connected waterways (called the Harris Chain of Lakes) over the years.

The Harris Chain was crucial to fisherman during the 1900s and was an essential route for the first settlers who used the lakes to transport goods back and forth to surrounding areas, such as the nearby town of Tavares. But the journey was not easy, and at night, it was practically impossible to navigate safe passage. The Mount Dora Lighthouse was built to aid the fishermen. Town members, traders, and elected officials all came together to raise the $3,000 required to build the lighthouse. Operation began on March 28, 1988, and "the little lighthouse that could" has been hard at work ever since. But there's even more to

Mount Dora and its lighthouse than meets the eye. That's right—even Central Florida is not safe from haunting!

Not only have spirits been spotted strolling in downtown Mount Dora, but visitors to the lighthouse have also reported hearing strange sounds at night. Skeptics blame these sounds on the wildlife that call Lake Dora home, including insects, birds, and even alligators. But that doesn't really explain the shadowy figures and other haunted apparitions that have been seen along the lake. When darkness falls, eerie lights seem to hover across the moonlit water. Some believe these specters may be ghosts of the fishermen and boaters who were not so lucky to have the illumination of Mount Dora Lighthouse to guide their way and perished as a result.

This part of Central Florida is still of great interest to supernatural enthusiasts and experts. Can its history offer a clue about its seemingly spooky future? That remains to be seen. But until such time, one thing is for sure: the hauntings at the lighthouse are not typical. Then again, neither is the Mount Dora Lighthouse.

Egmont Key Lighthouse

Egmont Key Lighthouse—located just south of St. Peterburg, Florida, in Egmont Key State Park—is said to be crawling with spirits of the dead.

Historians estimate Egmont Key to be thousands of years old, but the first activity recorded on the island was in 1757 with the arrival of Royal Spanish fleet pilot, Don

Francisco Maria Celi. Don Francisco named the island *La Isla de San Blas y Barreda*. Needless to say, that was a little long and didn't catch on.

When Florida became a British colony five years after Don Francisco's arrival, the island's name was changed to Egmont, after the Second Earl of Egmont, John Perceval. That name stuck.

During the Second Seminole War, from 1835 to 1842, this area was used as a detention center for captured Seminole soldiers. Many died in imprisonment. By 1848, construction on the first lighthouse structure began. But storms toppled the building almost as soon as it was completed. In September of that year, a hurricane forced the lighthouse keeper and his family to take shelter in a small boat tied to a nearby tree. When the waters calmed, they rowed all the way to Tampa, vowing never to return. The storm had drained their will, it had seemed.

Between 1848 and 1852, the lighthouse was hammered by three separate storms, causing considerable damage to the initial structure. Repairs were made in 1857, including an additional ninety feet added to the top of tower so that it could withstand hurricanes with more than a fighting chance.

The Second Seminole War would not be the last time the island was used as a place of detainment. Egmont Key was strategic in the American Civil War between the Confederate soldiers and the Union Army.

The Union Army detained confederate ships and imprisoned the soldiers. It was also used as a safe haven for pro-Union sympathizers.

In 1864, a cemetery was created at Egmont Key. It was maintained until the early 1900s. Then, over the course of time, the bodies were removed and distributed to different cemeteries throughout the country. Some locals believe this disturbance of the dead may have played a crucial role in setting loose the countless restless sprits of fallen soldiers.

One park ranger is certain he's seen a ghost of past conflicts on the island. One night, while going about his rounds, the ranger reported seeing a man dressed in a Confederate uniform walking not far from the lighthouse. This may not be the only spirit on the key. Shadowy figures disappear and reappear at the lighthouse base, and ghostly faces sometimes peer out of the lighthouse tower. What do you think? Would you be brave enough to step foot on the island at night?

Garden Key Light

Garden Key Light

You have probably heard tales of pirates searching for gold or seen movies involving someone's long-lost buried treasure. What if these stories were actually true, and riches galore were sitting at the bottom of the ocean, just waiting for discovery? Well, there *is* actually such a place! It's called Dry Tortugas National Park, on Garden Key, just a stone's throw away from Key West. The park is also home to Fort Jefferson and the Garden Key Light, which—if you haven't guessed by now—is home to many ghosts.

For such a tiny island, Garden Key has seen a lot of history. The name Dry Tortugas came from the famous Spanish explorer, Juan Ponce de León, who arrived at the island in 1513. Tortugas is the Spanish word for "turtles." At the time, there was a considerable population of sea turtles who called the inlets of Tortuga Harbor their home. "Dry" was added later to inform fishermen that the island lacked any freshwater sources to fish from.

And what about all the gold and riches? Well, in 1622, an event of great consequence occurred here. A fleet of Spanish treasure ships sank off the shores of the Florida Keys. These ships contained countless spoils, like gold, copper, diamonds, and olive jars. A deep-sea recovery team discovered what was believed to be the remains of these treasure-filled vessels in 1989. But could their presence, hundreds of years later, have disturbed something in the waters?

Possibly, but first you need to know about the events of 1742, when the crew of the British navy ship *Tyger* was marooned on the island for nearly sixty days. During that time, they struggled to survive with what resources they had. When the already-struggling members of the *Tyger* were attacked by enemy Spanish ships, they barely escaped with their lives by constructing improvised boats and sailing off to Jamaica as quickly as possible. This began what would continue to be a complicated time for the island.

Garden Key and its lighthouse, like so many islands and lighthouses in this region, played a pivotal role in the American Civil War. Fort Jefferson served as a base for a period, but more frequently, it was used as a prison—one that housed a very interesting physician: Dr. Samuel Mudd.

Dr. Mudd was sent to the prison on Fort Jefferson for conspiring with the assassin John Wilkes Boothe to kill President Abraham Lincoln. While Dr. Mudd was incarcerated, Fort Jefferson was in a state of havoc. Yellow fever, a deadly virus that killed many people of the era, was running rampant throughout the prison and surrounding areas. To Dr. Mudd, it appeared as though the military was dumping hundreds of dead bodies into the sea almost every day.

Perhaps he felt duty-bound as a physician, or maybe it was guilt over his role in the assassination of President Lincoln, but whatever inspired him, Dr. Mudd immediately got to work helping doctors and nurses contain the spread of yellow fever. For his efforts, guards at Fort Jefferson wrote letters to President Jackson detailing his help. Dr. Mudd was soon pardoned for his crimes and released.

As for the Garden Key Light, the structure itself is quite a marvel of its time. Made with more than sixty million bricks, this fortress in the Gulf is one of the largest brick structures in the United States. But make no mistake, it is quite haunted! Visitors and rangers at the park have claimed to witness shadow figures and ghosts behind nearly every corner. Sensitives—people who can sense the presence of the supernatural—have reported feeling a strange energy coming from the walls of the lighthouse and surrounding structures. Others tell spine-tingling tales of ghostly lights, spectral orbs, and a terrifying howl that echoes across the island in the dead of night. A howl some believe comes from the *devil* himself.

Most paranormal experts point to the many years this island was used as a prison as the reason for all the spooky activity. Whispers of cannibalism, beheadings, and cruel means of torture still linger today—though these are only rumors. Still, most people who come to camp out on Fort Jefferson Island seldom return. Could it be simply that the island is difficult to reach and offers few services? Or... might the island's restless spirits be keeping them away?

We may never know

for sure if Garden Key is haunted, but one thing remains certain: should you ever find yourself on a tour of the lighthouse, stay alert and listen carefully. That wind you hear howling... may not be the wind after all.

Ponce de Leon Inlet Light

Ten miles south of Daytona stands a world-famous lighthouse, the tallest in Florida. While climbing its 175-foot tower is certainly a challenge, those who manage the upward trek are treated to some of the greatest beauty that Mother Nature has to offer. Of course, the lighthouse we're talking about is the magnificent Ponce de Leon Inlet Light, which has been a shining standard on the Florida coast since 1888. Like the many other towering wonders in the Sunshine State, the Ponce de Leon Inlet Light is designated as a National Historic Landmark.

The tides of the Ponce de Leon Inlet have brought so much to these shores, from brutal storms to the pains of war. This area was once originally known as the Mosquito Inlet and was mostly populated by plantation owners. There were early attempts to construct a lighthouse, including a petition formed by the local community in 1830. But this attempt was fruitless and set in motion a series of peaks and valleys throughout the history of this region.

A forty-five-foot tower was initially built on the south side of the inlet between 1835 and 1836. But sadly, this beacon was never lit. The supply of oil that was meant to light the top chandelier never delivered, and weeks later a brutal storm struck the inlet, nearly killing lighthouse keeper William H. Williams and his family. Months later, the lighthouse was attacked by Seminole warriors. It seemed that anything that could happen to this tower *would* happen. In April 1836, another storm battered what was left of the southward structure and washed it completely into the ocean.

The inlet remained dark and relatively quiet for fifty years. Until 1887, when a brick structure was built—one of the last marvels of lighthouse masonry along the U.S. coastline. The new structure was a vast improvement over previous towers, and better still, it was fitted with one of the all-powerful Fresnel lenses. This is an important note in history, as it marks an era in time when lighthouses were made of brick, substantially improving the strength of the structures so they might sustain the storms, as well as casting more light than ever.

But since that time, bizarre occurrences have plagued this island and lighthouse with little explanation. Bartola Parcetta, who owned the land on which the lighthouse sits, died suddenly and was buried on the island. Then, just after the turn of the century, a significant number of whales began to wash up on the shore, dying or already dead. In 1919, lighthouse keeper, Joesph Davis, died here. Many believe he still haunts the lighthouse today, especially the staircase. Davis was working in the staircase tower when he suffered a heart attack and died.

Today, visitors report the distinct smell of kerosene in and around the area where Davis died. The smell is attributed to Davis's spirit, since kerosene hasn't been used to light the tower since 1933.

Could the scent signal the presence of Joseph Davis's spirit? It's anybody's guess. So brave reader, should you ever decide to visit the Ponce de Leon Inlet Light, be on the lookout—and always make sure to follow your nose!

Carysfort Reef Light

You've now read about many lighthouses and the history each one keeps inside their towers and surrounding grounds. You may have also noticed that the lighthouses served many different purposes over the course of their existence. Be it through war or natural disaster, lighthouses take their hits, and no structure is invincible, after all. This is certainly true of Carysfort Reef Light.

The current structure of Carysfort Reef Light sits comfortably just six nautical miles off Key Largo. It rises one hundred feet above the sea and was originally designed in an octagon-shaped pyramid. Named after the British navy ship, *Carysfort*, this first structure was built in New York City in 1825. It was then shipped by sea down the Atlantic coast, bound for Florida. But tragedy struck not long before it was due to reach its destination.

Near Key Biscayne, a storm rolled in and slammed the vessel—and the lighthouse—into the shoreline. Crewmen had no choice but to abandon the ship and its precious cargo. Deep sea wreckage teams were able to recover what was left of the ship, but the lighthouse structure would never be functional. Despite the best efforts of all involved, the structure was completely scrapped and rebuilt.

One lighthouse keeper, John Whalton, is

a crucial figure in the history of Carysfort Reef. Whalton was captain of the ship that carried the original lighthouse from New York to Florida, and he stayed on as charge of the lighthouse when it was replaced. These were especially unsettling times: after Seminole warriors burned down the Cape Florida Lighthouse, the Carysfort Reef Light was the only nautical marker between St. Augustine and Key West. Resources and manpower in the area were stretched thin. One day, Captain Whalton, along with a few of his assistants, went ashore to tend to one of their gardens at nearby Garden Cove. They were attacked by a Seminole army. Whalton and one of his assistants were killed, while two narrowly escaped by boat to safety.

It seems, though, that the spirit of Captain Whalton is still a consistent presence in the ruins of the lighthouse he once called home.

The lighthouse was officially decommissioned for use in 2015 and has been described as a "floating skeleton," like something from a horror movie. Its metal and steel remains are rusted out completely, groaning and creaking eerily as the wind whistles through. The surrounding waters are infested with hungry sharks, while hidden reefs and a sandbar make navigating the shallows nearly impossible. In other words, it's the perfect place for a ghost to hang out!

Many locals claim that when the sun sets on the lighthouse in the evening, terrifying sounds like shrieks, moans, and even howls can be heard in the wind—as if the place is possessed by ghosts or demons, or both. Many believe this is the sound of Captain Whalton's widow, mourning the loss of her beloved husband. Want to know what's even creepier? Some say they have even spotted the ghost of Captain Whalton throughout the area! Paranormal experts believe that he may be caught in a supernatural loop. This happens when spirits traveling from one world to the next become trapped, reliving their last days over and over. In the case of Captain Whalton, he may be reliving the fatal attack by the Seminoles.

Skeptics say that those who claim to have seen ghosts are just suffering from delusions brought on by dehydration. Talk about being crazy from the Florida heat! But skepticism aside, whatever is still lingering here has clearly made its presence known. Whether it's spectral keepers, ghostly pirates, or Captain Whalton himself, the spirits of Carysfort Reef Light are practically hiding in plain sight. Or, could people just be seeing things that aren't really there?

Note to self: stay hydrated on your lighthouse tour of Florida!

A Ghostly Goodbye

Now that you've learned about the incredible lighthouses of Florida and have dived deep into the history that surrounds them, do you still believe they could be haunted? Are you sold on the idea of paranormal existence? Is there an active afterlife for everyone to look forward to someday?

Or... is there another lesson to be learned here, which is that people often stand in the way of the greatness a lighthouse offers, lost in their wars and their indifference to Mother Nature? Regardless, be sure to make time to visit these miraculous manmade creations. They have kept the seas safe for hundreds of years and will likely continue to do so for hundreds more.

In the end, one thing is clear: these towers each have a life and story of their own to tell. Stop by sometime and have a listen.

Dan Alleva is an author, editor, and journalist from Brooklyn, New York. You can read his daily news stories from the world of music online at Metal Injection, and find some of his truly hilarious *Mad Libs* titles in your favorite local bookstore. When not writing, Dan can be found rooting on his beloved Manchester United with his incredible daughter, Olivia.

Check out some of the other *Spooky America* titles available now!

Spooky America was adapted from the creeptastic *Haunted America* series for adults. *Haunted America* explores historical haunts in cities and regions across America. Here's more from the original *Ghosts and Legends of Florida Pirates* author, Heather Leigh, PhD:

 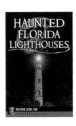  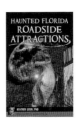